Y0-BZE-386
A85500 045120

At 11:00 P.M. on the night of August 20, 1968, Soviet, Polish, Hungarian, East German, and Bulgarian troops invaded the Czechoslovak Socialist Republic. Within hours, Czechoslovakia's top leaders had been captured and flown to Moscow. This invasion of a nation at peace was carried out in the name of "socialist solidarity." The real reasons for the invasion were far more complex. During the eight months from January to August, 1968, the Czechoslovaks had put an end to twenty years of strict Communist rule. In its place they had tried to create a form of "socialism with a human face" and briefly enjoyed freedom of speech, the press, and travel. The eight-month experiment ended in the shadow of "fraternal" Communist tanks, probably because the Soviet Union feared that Czechoslovakia's experiment in freedom might spread like a disease through all of Communist Eastern Europe and the U.S.S.R.

PRINCIPALS

THE CZECHOSLOVAKS

Klement Gottwald (1896–1953), first Communist leader of Czechoslovak People's Democracy founded in 1948. A strict upholder of Stalin's views.

Antonín Novotný (1904–), Gottwald's successor as party first secretary and later also president. Replaced in 1968 by Dubček as first secretary and Svoboda as president.

Alexander Dubček (1921–), Slovak-born first secretary of the party during Czechoslovakia's eight-month experiment in establishing a freer form of communism.

Gustav Husák (1913–), Slovak intellectual and longtime Communist, who succeeded Dubček as first secretary of the party in 1969.

General Ludvík Svoboda (1895–), served under Soviet colors in World War II, replaced Novotný in 1968 as president, and supported Dubček until his fall. Stayed on as figurehead of pro-Soviet government.

THE RUSSIANS AND THEIR ALLIES

Leonid I. Brezhnev (1906–), general secretary of the Communist party in the U.S.S.R. at the time of the invasion.

Aleksei N. Kosygin (1904–), premier of the U.S.S.R. in 1968.

János Kadár (1912–), first secretary of the Central Committee of the Hungarian Communist party and head of the Hungarian Politburo.

Walter Ulbricht (1893–), Communist leader of the German Democratic Republic who strongly opposed Dubček's experiment with a freer form of socialism.

Władysław Gomułka (1905–), Polish Communist leader at the time of the invasion.

THE INVASION OF CZECHOSLOVAKIA

AUGUST, 1968
The End of a Socialist Experiment in Freedom

By Tad Szulc

A World Focus Book

FRANKLIN WATTS, INC.
NEW YORK | 1974

This book is for Hania

Frontispiece: Prague, August 21, 1968. A Czechoslovak holds a flag stained with the blood of one of his countrymen as Warsaw Pact tanks roll by.

Picture Credits

Eastfoto: p. 22 top, p. 30, p. 42 bottom, p. 47 top (Renato Perez), p. 47 bottom, p. 53, p. 58, p. 60.
Joachim Messerschmidt, Free Lance Photographers Guild: p. 42 top.
Keystone Pictures, Inc.: p. 26.
Pace Public Relations: p. 17 (Joseph Ehm), p. 34.
Wide World Photos: frontis, p. vi, p. 6, p. 22 bottom, p. 50.

Cover by Hautrive Graphics
Map by Danmark & Michaels
Photo research by Selma Hamdan

Library of Congress Cataloging in Publication Data

Szulc, Tad.
The invasion of Czechoslovakia, August, 1968.

(A World focus book)
Bibliography: p.
SUMMARY: Discusses the events behind Czechoslovakia's 1968 invasion by five fellow Communist countries.
1. Czechoslovak Republic–History–Intervention, 1968– –Juvenile literature. [1. Czechoslovak Republic–History–Intervention, 1968] I. Title.
DB215.6.S98 943.7'04 73-12072
ISBN 0-531-02172-6

Printed in the United States of America
6 5 4 3 2 1

Contents

Young Czechs pried cobblestones out of the streets to hurl at the invading troops in August, 1968.

The Peacetime Invasion

At 11:00 P.M. on the muggy night of Tuesday, August 20, 1968, long columns of Soviet, Polish, Hungarian, East German, and Bulgarian troops invaded Czechoslovakia. The invading troops, spearheaded by tank units, penetrated four borders of that small Communist Central European country. At the same time, Soviet transport aircraft, led by sleek MIG jet fighters, began landing with high precision at the Prague and Bratislava airports to unload paratroopers and airborne troops. By the time the sun rose over the stunned capital, Prague, the top leaders of Czechoslovakia had been captured. They were being flown to Moscow, handcuffed and under armed military guard.

This peacetime invasion of Czechoslovakia by the Soviet Union and four of its partners in the Warsaw Pact military alliance was carried out in the name of "socialist solidarity." It was designed to smash the experiment in creating a form of "Socialism with a Human Face" that had been launched in Czechoslovakia, also a Warsaw Pact member, in January, 1968. For nearly eight months progressive-minded Communists had led this experiment. It revolved around the idea that such political and human liberties as freedom of speech and a free press could flourish in a Marxist system. But the experiment had been watched with growing concern by the Communist leaders in the Soviet Union, Poland, and East Germany. The Hungarians, whose own revolution against strict Communist controls had been flattened by Soviet tanks in 1956, reluctantly joined this "police action." The only Warsaw Pact member that refused to participate was Rumania.

Nothing like the peacetime invasion of Czechoslovakia had ever taken place in the relations between the Soviet Union and its Communist allies in Europe. When the Soviet Union moved against Poland and Hungary in 1956, there had been violent uprisings in the streets. But Czechoslovakia was completely at peace during the summer of 1968. Many of its citizens were away on vacations in the mountains, at their country cottages, or even abroad—since the new government had lifted the ban on foreign travel. The Czechoslovaks seemed confident that their experiment would survive. Only three weeks earlier, the Warsaw Pact leaders had met with the Czechoslovak leaders in the city of Bratislava to proclaim a new era of friendship.

Looking back at the events of 1968, it seems quite clear that the sudden attack was inevitable. It had been known for months that Warsaw Pact troops were massing on Czechoslovak borders. The Russians had even held military maneuvers in Czechoslovakia in the weeks before the invasion. It seems clear now that Moscow believed it was necessary to marshal at least a quarter of a million troops to kill the spread of ideas that it found unacceptable in a fellow Communist country.

In fact, it is now known that when the invading armies burst into Czechoslovakia, all the advance preparations in the country already had been completed. On August 17, when the Czechoslovak Communist leader Alexander Dubček was meeting the Hungarian leader, János Kadár, a Soviet airliner landed in Prague. On board was a team of specialists from the KGB, the Soviet secret police. They immediately established liaison with the Soviet embassy and a group of men in the Interior Ministry who were loyal to Moscow. These were the men who quietly kept alive a pro-Soviet security apparatus during the experiment to develop a new kind of socialism. The apparatus was designed to be activated if, and when, an invasion came.

On August 20 Dubček called a meeting of the party's Presidium to review the situation in the light of the letter he had received from Leonid Brezhnev, the general secretary of the Soviet Communist party. Curiously, however, Dubček did not seem to interpret this letter as the virtual announcement of the invasion that Brezhnev must have meant it to be. And, just as the Presidium was meeting in the Central Commitee building overlooking the Vltava River, Czechoslovak and Soviet security agents were gathering at the Interior Ministry to plan their actions in the coming hours. Orders were issued for the arrest of the progressive leaders of the party and for the take-over of radio and television stations.

On August 20 at 10:30 P.M., two Soviet airliners landed at Prague's

Ruzyń airport. One was parked at the far end of the field to serve as a mobile control tower to direct the Soviet airlift that was about to start. A contingent of Soviet officers in civilian clothes came out of the other plane. They formed the advance command team. It was these men who secured the airport terminal and rushed to the Soviet embassy to coordinate the steps in the invasion.

Dubček and the Presidium were still in session when, at the stroke of 11:00 P.M., Soviet and other Warsaw Pact units crossed the Czechoslovakian border at twelve points. Huge transport aircraft started landing at the Prague and Bratislava airports to unload airborne combat troops. The Soviet ambassador drove to Hradčany Castle to inform Czechoslovakia's President Ludvík Svoboda that "fraternal" forces had invaded the country in the name of "socialist solidarity." A pro-Soviet official of the Czechoslovak Communist party appeared at the offices of the national news agency with the text of an announcement that the foreign troops had been "invited" into Czechoslovakia by unnamed "patriotic" leaders. But—in the first of many acts of defiance to the invaders—the agency refused to transmit the message to the outside world.

The Presidium learned of the invasion at 11:40 P.M. when Premier Oldřich Černík received a telephone call from the Defense Ministry. When he heard the news Dubček, with tears in his eyes, said: "I declare on my honor as a Communist I had no suspicion, no indication, that anyone would want to undertake such measures against us." Then he added: "That they should have done this to me, after I dedicated my whole life to cooperation with the Soviet Union, is the greatest tragedy of my life."

But Dubček recovered quickly and ordered the drafting of a message to the Czechoslovak people. Shortly after midnight the population was informed over the radio (which the security agents had failed to capture) that the party Presidium considered the invasion "to be contrary to the fundamental principles of relations between Socialist states and a denial of basic forms of international law." The proclamation also urged the armed forces and the population to refrain from resistance "because the defense of our state borders is now impossible." Nevertheless, the Presidium's statement marked the beginning of passive resistance that was to continue for long months. Without firing a shot, the Czechoslovaks had begun to upset the carefully calculated Soviet timetable for the occupation of their country.

The military part of the timetable moved with precision. Shortly before 5:00 A.M. on August 21, Soviet tanks occupied the bridges over the Vltava, thus cutting the city into two parts. Tanks surrounded all the strategic points in the capital. Significantly, these strategic points included the headquarters of the Writers' Union, the Journalists' Union, and the Academy of Sciences. These were the places where the ideas had been born that led to the invasion of Czechoslovakia.

Other tank units surrounded the party's Central Committee building, the Council of Ministers building, and Hradčany Castle, the seat of government. Dubček and three other leaders were arrested by Soviet officers at the party headquarters. Premier Černík was taken at his office in the Council of Ministers building. All five were immediately taken to an unknown destination. The aging President Svoboda was allowed to remain as a virtual prisoner at Hradčany.

The invasion was a textbook operation and, in the absence of organized military resistance, it succeeded brilliantly. Only a brief battle around Wenceslaus Square in the heart of Prague over the control of the Prague Radio building produced bloodshed and casualties. There were a few later incidents in Prague and elsewhere. But the death toll among the Czechoslovaks did not exceed about thirty killed and three hundred wounded. The Russians lost a few tanks that the angry youths in Prague succeeded in setting on fire during the battle for the radio station.

But almost a week was to elapse before the threat of a major massacre finally was removed. This was because—to the Russians' complete surprise—the political part of their invasion failed just as totally as the military operation succeeded. Contrary to Soviet expectations,

President Svoboda refused to accept a new cabinet that the Soviet ambassador submitted to him the day after the invasion. The old general even haughtily informed the Russians that he would have no dealings with them as long as Dubček and his companions remained imprisoned in Moscow. And, finally, the Soviet embassy could not find enough respectable Communists, even among the conservatives, to form a new party leadership. With this, the fiction that the invasion was ordered in response to an "invitation" from Prague crumbled at once.

Among those who questioned this fiction—and took a horrified view of Moscow's actions—were the big Western European Communist parties. The Italian party condemned the invasion out of hand. The French party split right down the middle over the invasion. Its younger and more liberal officials and members bitterly denounced Moscow. The small but important British party also denounced the invasion. China, Yugoslavia, and Rumania—always fearful of Soviet intentions—protested the Czech adventure. Curiously, the tiny Communist party of the United States lined up unquestioningly behind the Kremlin.

As a result of the Czechoslovak and foreign reactions to the invasion, the Soviet Union found itself in the extraordinary position of having to negotiate with the remaining leaders of the country it had just occupied militarily. A government had to be created in Prague—the Russians were not prepared to establish their own military government—but this could not be done so long as Moscow kept the Czechoslovak leaders in prison. It was an incredible stalemate.

The situation was complicated even more by the amazing spirit of Czechoslovak passive resistance. It was one of the vital factors that Soviet planning had failed to take into account. No sooner had the Soviet tanks captured the Prague radio station than an underground broadcasting network sprang up under the noses of the occupiers. Transmitting from secret locations in Prague and all the large Czechoslovak cities, the underground radio kept the population informed of all developments. It broadcast defiant proclamations by President

TEPLICE
LETŇANY

Svoboda and the texts of hundreds of resolutions by workers and students demanding the release of the leaders in Moscow. Before long, the secret network was able to add television transmissions from underground studios to its around-the-clock radio operation.

Despite the presence of Soviet troops, newspapers were published underground in one-page editions to denounce the occupation. The Russians were left without a voice in Czechoslovakia except for a radio station broadcasting in Czech from East Germany and a military newspaper that no Czechoslovak cared to read. When Soviet troops distributed copies of *Pravda,* the Soviet Communist party's newspaper, people burned them in the streets.

On August 22, the Czechoslovak Communist party managed to hold a secret congress at an industrial plant in Prague. Despite Soviet precautions, delegates were able to reach the congress disguised as morning-shift workers. The plant's militia and security services were protecting the congress. At the day's end, the congress reelected the absent Dubček as first secretary and named an overwhelmingly liberal Central Committee. It is quite possible that this immense show of solidarity saved the lives of Dubček and his four companions. There are reasons to believe that the Russians were considering executing them. This, in turn, would have led to a bloody explosion in Prague.

Moscow had no choice but to negotiate. On August 23, President Svoboda agreed to fly to the Soviet capital for talks with the Kremlin leaders. His principal aim was to win the captives' freedom. But, obviously, the political situation had to be discussed, too.

A war of nerves was fought during the next four days. In Prague, pro-Dubček demonstrations served to strengthen Svoboda's negotiating position. The Russians countered by deploying artillery around the capital. It was absolutely clear that they were prepared to level Prague if an agreement could not be reached in Moscow. At the Kremlin, Svoboda threatened public suicide if Dubček and the others were not set free.

To confuse the invaders, Czechoslovakians painted signs with "useful" directions to "Dubček" and "Moscow."

Finally, the Soviet Union compromised. The hostages were released and allowed to participate in the negotiations. An accord was reached under which Soviet troops would remain indefinitely in Czechoslovakia—or until "normalization" of the situation had been achieved. But Dubček was allowed to stay on as the party's first secretary and Černík as premier.

When Svoboda and his group returned to Prague on August 27, they brought back a remarkable victory—considering the circumstances. Both the party leadership and the government remained intact. It was an amazing feat in the light of the fact that the Russians had invaded Czechoslovakia in order to remove these very men from power. To be sure, the power the Prague leaders were now free to exercise had considerable limits. The experiment in "Marxism with a Human Face" could no longer go on. But the central fact was that the Russians were unable to impose a puppet government on Czechoslovakia, and years were to go by before the spirit of resistance finally wore down.

Why Invasion?

Why did the Soviet Union decide to risk staging a major military invasion in the heartland of a peaceful Europe? Why did the Soviet Union choose to sacrifice the years of improvement in its relationships with the West, especially the United States?

For example, the invasion forced the cancellation of a new planned "summit" meeting between Lyndon B. Johnson, then president of the United States, and the Soviet premier, Aleksei Kosygin. Although the United States government obviously had been aware of Soviet military preparations, the actual invasion took it by surprise. In Washington, President Johnson learned of it from the Soviet ambassador, Anatoly F. Dobrynin, who called on him at the White House by well-timed prearrangement to say that the move into Czechoslovakia was not meant to threaten U. S. interests. Because of the time difference, it was just a few minutes before 5:00 P.M. in Washington when the ambassador delivered his message. Secretary of State Dean Rusk, busy testifying before the Democratic party's foreign policy platform committee at the national convention in Chicago, learned of the invasion when a wire service flash was handed to him. He read it aloud as television cameras were focused on him.

Halfway around the world the invasion also caused an important change. We now know that the invasion of Czechoslovakia was perhaps the single most important factor in convincing mainland China, then emerging from the turmoil of the Great Proletarian Cultural Revolution, that it needed to seek links with the United States. This process climaxed with President Richard Nixon's historic visit to Peking in 1972. The Chinese seem to have decided that they could not remain isolated in the world at a time when the Russians—deeply at odds with them since 1958—had shown themselves capable of invading a Communist nation whose politics they abhorred. In fact, the talk in those days, and afterward, was of an imminent Soviet "first strike" nuclear attack on China's own atomic arsenal.

What persuaded the Kremlin that the Czechoslovak invasion was worth such risks and hostile reactions?

In the first place, it must be remembered that Czechoslovakia geographically is the westernmost of the European Communist nations. Its territory, shaped like a long arrow, juts out of Eastern Europe into Central Europe. Its western frontiers adjoin neutral but pro-Western Austria as well as West Germany in which the North Atlantic Treaty Organization (NATO) and the United States maintain armies of over half a million men. In 1968, Czechoslovakia was the only Warsaw Pact nation, aside from Rumania, deep in Communist East Europe, that refused the permanent stationing of Soviet troops in its territory.

Moscow's official argument for the invasion was that the quickening liberalization in Czechoslovakia under the direction of Alexander Dubček, the immensely popular first secretary of the Communist party, threatened the military security of the Warsaw Pact bloc. The

Russians suspected Dubček and his outspoken colleagues—even old President Svoboda—of "neutralism" and pro-Western sympathies. They worried aloud about Czechoslovakia's plans to shift to a less centrally controlled economy. The U.S.S.R. wanted Czechoslovakia to have a tightly controlled state economy linked to the Soviet Union, just as it had been since 1948. Moscow also expressed fears that the 200,000-man Czechoslovak army would collapse before a Western onslaught, which would threaten all of Communist East Europe. After all, the old saying was that he who controls Bohemia and Moravia—the historic heart of Czechoslovakia—will control Europe.

There is no reason to believe that the West ever had the slightest idea of invading Czechoslovakia to take advantage of Dubček's alleged "weakness." But it obviously served Soviet purposes to charge, as Moscow did daily, that Americans and West Germans were engaged in sinister conspiracies against the safety of the Communist states. Czechoslovakia, Poland, and East Germany were known as the "Iron Triangle" in the defense of the East against the West—and Moscow saw, or thought it saw, one of the sides of this triangle crumbling before its very eyes.

This, then, was the official script for invading and, thereby, "saving" Czechoslovakia from the West.

Yet there were stronger, if unspoken, reasons for the Kremlin to order hundreds of thousands of troops, equipped with tactical battlefield nuclear weapons, into Czechoslovakia in that hot August week—a week when Czechoslovak farmers were peacefully harvesting their rich fields and the sun bathed Prague's golden domes and spires.

Among these unspoken reasons was the Soviet concern that the success of Dubček's experiment in granting freedoms—if allowed to go on unchecked—might undermine the entire political structure in Eastern Europe. They feared that it might even threaten stability within the Soviet Union.

Liberty, as the Russians well understood, can be highly dangerous, explosive, and contagious. So can nationalism. This, then, could have been a lethal combination menacing the political, ideological,

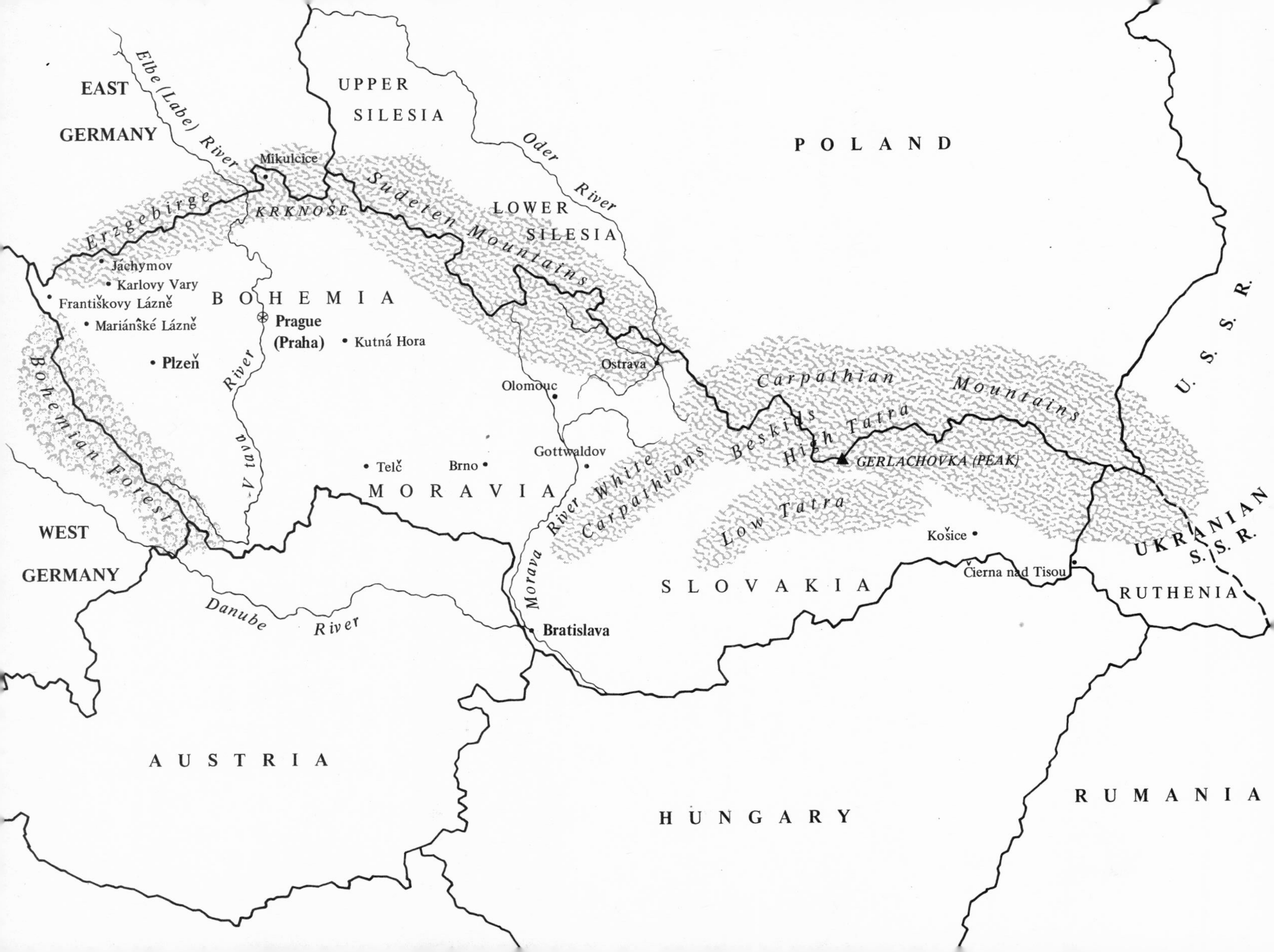
EAST
GERMANY
Elbe (Labe) River
UPPER
SILESIA
POLAND
Oder River
LOWER
SILESIA
Mikulcice
Erzgebirge
KRKNOŠE
Sudeten Mountains
Jáchymov
Karlovy Vary
Františkovy Lázně
Mariánské Lázně
BOHEMIA
Prague
(Praha)
Kutná Hora
Plzeň
Bohemian Forest
V tava River
Ostrava
Olomouc
Gottwaldov
Telč
Brno
MORAVIA
Morava River
White Carpathians
Carpathian Mountains
Beskids
High Tatra
GERLACHOVKA (PEAK)
Low Tatra
Košice
Čierna nad Tisou
SLOVAKIA
U. S. S. R.
UKRANIAN S. S. R.
RUTHENIA
WEST
GERMANY
Danube River
Bratislava
AUSTRIA
HUNGARY
RUMANIA

economic, and military system the Kremlin had so painstakingly constructed in Eastern Europe after World War II.

This system consists of the Communist party rule in Poland, East Germany, Czechoslovakia, Bulgaria, and Rumania. In each country the Soviet Union operates as if it were the "chairman of the board." The ultimate decision-maker in vital affairs in each of these nations is the Soviet Union.

Politically, these regimes reflect the intimate meshing of the Communist party and the executive and legislative branches in each country. Although organizational details may vary, the undisputed leader in every case is the head of the local party. He has the title of first secretary, general secretary, or secretary-general. In some instances, the party leader may also wear the hat of the premier and be directly responsible for the functioning of the government. In other cases, the premier is subordinated to the party leader.

In every East European Communist nation, the most powerful body is the Political Bureau—the Politburo—of the party's Central Committee. The cabinet ministers form a lower level in running a nation's affairs. Often they are figureheads but, on occasion, a Politburo member may also be in the cabinet. Permanent secretaries of the Central Committee outrank cabinet ministers as a practical matter, although there are overlaps. In size, the Politburo may vary from eight to as many as sixteen members. In almost every case, the president of the republic is a figurehead—approved by the Politburo or even a member of this body—but at different times the party's top leader may also act as president: this was the case of Antonín Novotný in Czechoslovakia and Nicolae Ceaușescu in Rumania.

Militarily, the system is built around the Soviet armed forces. The Warsaw Pact alliance, under Soviet direction, acts as a regional command patterned after NATO. Economically, the Soviet Union, the Eastern European countries, and Outer Mongolia are joined in the Council for Mutual Economic Assistance. Known as COMECON, it is somewhat like Western Europe's Common Market. In COMECON, too, Moscow is the senior partner. The alliance controls the economic life of the 300 million people in Eastern Europe. The result for a highly industrialized nation like Czechoslovakia is almost disastrous because its goods are sold at prices set by Moscow, rather than what they would earn in a competitive world market.

But both this Soviet-led political system and the "leading role" of the Communist parties in Eastern Europe have repeatedly been challenged from within. In most cases the Soviet Union moved firmly to restore stability. The Soviet Union used tanks to end a workers' rebellion in East Berlin in 1953. It halted a surge of liberalism in Poland in 1956 by bringing army divisions to the outskirts of Warsaw. And, a few months later, a Hungarian revolt was drowned in blood as Soviet armor swept down the streets of Budapest.

Twice, however, Moscow was unable to prevent Communist countries from breaking free of the system. The first time was in 1948. In that year, Marshal Tito, who cared more about his nation's welfare than about Communist unity, removed Yugoslavia from the Soviet sphere of influence. The Russians chose not to risk what might have been a new European war to keep Yugoslavia in the fold. In 1961, tiny Albania turned away from the Soviet Union to enter into an alliance with faraway China, the Russians' principal enemy.

For two decades, then, the constant Soviet preoccupation in Eastern Europe—from the Baltic Sea in the north to the Adriatic Sea in the south—was with the preservation of political unity. This meant that all the nations forming the bloc must pay allegiance to basic Soviet policies and interests. For this to be achieved, Moscow had to be satisfied that in each case the local Communist party was fully in control at home and that it unquestioningly accepted the Kremlin's leadership. Thus a uniform political pattern had to be imposed on this bloc rich in different nationalities, tongues, and cultures.

Having painstakingly built up this system in East Europe, the Kremlin is alert to the dangers of nationalist contagion in the region. This is because each surge of independence or liberalism has seemed to set off a sympathy movement next door, often within the Soviet Union itself.

For example, the Russians reasoned that nationalist stirrings in Ukraine (a vast Soviet republic adjoining Czechoslovakia and Poland) and in such other Soviet areas as Latvia, Lithuania, and the Caucasus could be further encouraged by uncontrolled independence movements in Eastern Europe. Growing demands for freedom by Soviet intellectuals seemed to be closely linked to Eastern European rebellions directed by local intellectuals.

Thus, when the Czechoslovak experiment in liberal Communism —fed by nationalist demands and powerful intellectual and political dissent against the practices of the past—erupted in 1968, the Soviet Union immediately was faced by what it saw as a basic threat to its interests.

In fact, Czechoslovakia seemed to offer every possible element of danger to the East European unity and stability that was so vital to Moscow.

Czechoslovakia's basic national feeling was not only anti-Russian. The republic's population of fourteen and one-half million is made up of several different national groups. The Slovaks, who live in the eastern third of the country, speak a separate Slav language. They demanded a larger degree of self-government. In addition, there is a large Hungarian minority in eastern Slovakia, creating a nationalist problem of its own. Along the eastern frontier there are Ruthenians who feel closer to the Ukrainians than to the Czechs. This assortment of nationalist problems in Czechoslovakia was disturbing to Moscow, especially if it was going to be allowed to go on by the government in Prague.

Another fact the Russians could never forget was that the Czechs were the most Western-minded people in the region. They had closer ties to Western intellectual and industrial traditions than to those of the East. Perhaps more than other Eastern Europeans, they were open and receptive to the West's ideas. In fact, it took a Moscow-engineered coup d'état—overthrow of the government—in 1948 to turn Czechoslovakia into a Communist state. This was three years after the other Eastern European nations had been liberated by the Soviet armies from Nazi Germany's rule and Communist governments had been set up. Thus, for three years after the war, as well as in the decade before the war, Czechoslovakia was a Western democracy. This experience was not to be forgotten in the years that followed.

Still another vital fact in Moscow's view was that Czechoslovakia was vital to the East European economy. Its highly developed industry and its mineral resources, including uranium, were indispensable to the COMECON bloc and to the Soviet Union, which drew extensively on Czechoslovakia's production of industrial equipment, manufactured goods, and minerals. And, the Czechs also had one of Europe's best armaments industries. Czechoslovakia simply could not be lost to the bloc.

Despite these facts, which now seem so obvious, in August, 1968, the Czechoslovaks were still confident that they would never be invaded by the Soviet Union. "This is not Budapest in 1956," they said. "This is twelve years later. We have peace at home. And the Russians, too, have changed. They are very much concerned with their image in the world."

What proved the Czechoslovaks wrong on the night of August 20 was the logic of Russian, or Soviet, history. The situation in Czechoslovakia, with liberal and pro-Western sentiment mounting every hour, had convinced the Kremlin that the Dubček experiment could not go on any longer. It became clear that the Russians were much more concerned with Czechoslovakia and the danger of letting its liberal experiment go on freely than they were with their world "image."

Stunned as the Czechs and Slovaks were by the lightning invasion, they fought back as well as they could—in their very special way. Any organized resistance by the Czechoslovak armed forces would have been suicidal and, therefore, there was none. Actually, President Svoboda told his troops not to resist even before the first Soviet tanks reached Hradčany Castle. But a remarkable spirit of national resistance immediately sprang up.

On the first day, August 21, Czech men and women fought against

Soviet tanks in the center of Prague to prevent the Russians from capturing the building of Radio Prague which, from the first moment, became the center of resistance. Tanks were set on fire, but the Soviet power was overwhelming and, quickly, cannon and machine gun fire dispersed the crowds.

In the days, weeks, and months to come, the artful Czechoslovak resistance astounded the Russians—and the world. But, inevitably, Soviet power and the passage of time finally eroded most of the Czechoslovak resistance. Whether the spirit of rebellion has died down altogether, only the future and history can tell. But 1968 was the year of courage and glory for which the nation had waited so long.

The Years of Waiting

History rarely has been kind to the Czechoslovaks. Their great ventures and enterprises have always seemed doomed to tragic defeat. Their noble and courageous ideas have always seemed to lead to bitter disenchantment.

An important reason for this historical tragedy is the geographic location of the Czech lands at the crossroads of Europe. Central Europe could not be dominated without the control of Bohemia and Moravia. These lands also were a barrier against Muslim invasions in the Middle Ages and, later, both a wall and a bridge between East and West. The Czech lands, then, were always a battlefield in the wars of others, or a precious strategic prize to be captured and kept.

The Czechs, a Slav tribe, settled the region in about the sixth century A.D. They developed their own distinctive Slavic language and a clear sense of nationality. The nation's first martyr to the ambitions of stronger men was the tenth-century ruler, Wenceslaus I. He was murdered on the orders of his brother—partly because of his emphasis

A statue of St. Wenceslaus in downtown Prague. The tenth-century ruler is revered as the nation's first martyr.

on spreading Christianity, and partly because he encouraged neighboring German-speaking people to settle in and help develop the Czech lands. To this day the Czechs revere the memory of Saint Wenceslaus. And, almost to this day, the nation has been wracked by religious conflicts and victimized by the ambitions of its powerful German-speaking neighbors.

In the late thirteenth century when the Habsburg rulers were establishing themselves in Austria, they defeated the Czech king Ottokar II, who had built up a large empire in Central Europe. The empire was dismantled by the Habsburgs, marking the beginning of their long involvement in Czech life.

The devoutly Roman Catholic Habsburgs of Austria were among the first to recognize the threat presented by the first great Protestant reformer, a fifteenth-century Czech named John Huss. Huss preached against the great wealth of the Roman Catholic Church and urged a return to the simpler ways of the early Church. He also helped to keep Czech national feeling alive by preaching his sermons in Czech rather than Church Latin, and arguing that schools should use the Czech language as well. Huss's nationalism and his advocacy of reform are part of a long Czech tradition that came to life again in 1968. And, like his twentieth-century successors, Huss was punished severely. He was brought to trial and burned at the stake as a heretic in 1415. Nevertheless, the wave of reform he had begun and the national feeling he had helped keep alive were not so easily erased.

The Habsburgs managed to establish their rule over the Czech lands in 1526. It lasted for nearly four centuries and ultimately involved such extreme measures as making German the only official language of the nation and ending Czech self-government. Even so, the flame of Czech resistance kept flaring up. The Czechs rose against their Habsburg overlords in the seventeenth century, during the savage contest for the succession to the Austrian throne that became the Thirty Years' War. The war began in 1618 when Czech patriots protested Austrian rule by simply throwing a few Austrian officials out of a window at Hradčany Castle. This event, which is known to history as the Defenestration in Prague, led to the Battle of White Mountain in 1620. The Czechs were quickly defeated by the larger Austrian army but the Austrians were still not satisfied. In 1621 twenty-seven nobles were executed by the Habsburgs in Prague. It was a clear warning that anyone suspected of Protestant and anti-Habsburg beliefs would be dealt with in a similar fashion.

One result was an exodus of Czech nobles and leaders to other, freer European countries. Among the approximately thirty thousand exiles was the outstanding Czech Protestant bishop and teacher Jan Amos Komenský (Comenius). A martyr to his beliefs, as Huss had been before him, Komenský had also urged the use of Czech in place of Latin in schools and churches, and advocated such then revolutionary ideas as that education should be related to everyday life.

The loss of such leaders as Komenský had a serious effect on Czech national life. It was not until the early nineteenth century that there was a rebirth of interest in the ancient traditions of the country. This interest blossomed in many different ways—new histories were written about the half-forgotten past and old traditions were reborn and found their way into the music, art, and literature of the nation. Even the Czech language took on its modern form as the result of the work of linguists and grammarians whose forerunners had been men like Huss and Komenský. Politically, the Czechs and the Slovaks were locked into the Austro-Hungarian Empire. The industries of Bohemia grew rapidly to become some of the most important in Europe. And Czech representatives to the parliament in Vienna played a role in liberalizing the ancient Habsburg institutions of government. It is clear now that these Czech politicians were gently edging the empire toward its ultimate disintegration.

When World War I began in 1914, Czech and Slovak patriots chose to fight alongside the allied armies in France and Russia against Austria and Germany. In the United States, Tomáš Garrigue Masaryk, an exiled Czech professor, campaigned for a free Czechoslovakia. In 1918, Czechoslovakia—with the backing of the American president, Woodrow Wilson—emerged as an independent nation from the ruins of the Austro-Hungarian Empire. Masaryk became its first president.

Under Masaryk and his successor, Eduard Beneš, Czechoslovakia enjoyed a twenty-year period–its only one–of complete freedom and relative prosperity. More than any of the other new European states, Czechoslovakia had a full-fledged political democracy – even the Communist party functioned legally. Its industry continued to grow and became the most important in Central Europe aside from Germany's.

In Czechoslovakia, alas, it seems that nothing good ever lasts very long. In 1938, as the clouds of a new war gathered over Europe, Adolf Hitler demanded that the Sudetenland, the westernmost portion of Czechoslovakia, which had a large German ethnic population, be annexed to Nazi Germany. Hitler already had grabbed the Rhineland–the coal- and steel-producing area of what is now West Germany and then was a French protectorate–and Austria without opposition from the West. Although President Beneš was prepared to resist and went as far as to mobilize his army, the West let him down.

On September 30, 1938, Britain's prime minister, Neville Chamberlain, and France's premier, Edouard Daladier, flew to Munich to meet with Hitler and his partner, the Italian Fascist leader, Benito Mussolini. The result, which Chamberlain called "peace in our time," was that Czechoslovakia was to give the Sudetenland to Germany because Britain and France would not fight for her. According to Chamberlain, there was no point in going to war "because of a quarrel in a faraway country between people of whom we know nothing." Hitler said the Sudetenland was his "last territorial ambition in Europe." Beneš bitterly told his cabinet that "they decided about us, without us." Poland wasted no time helping herself to Czechoslovakia's Lower Silesia, and Hungary took a slice of southeastern Slovakia. The republic was dismembered.

Six months later, in March, 1939, Nazi troops marched unopposed into Prague. The Nazi propaganda chief declared, "Czechoslovakia has ceased to exist." Hitler created a puppet state in Slovakia, hoping to win some advantage from Slovak nationalism. Beneš fled to London to establish a Czechoslovak government-in-exile. "Peace in our time" lasted until September 1, 1939, when Hitler invaded Poland. World War II was underway.

Between 1941, when the Allies recognized the exiled Beneš government, and 1945, the postwar future of Czechoslovakia was a matter of rivalry between Czechoslovak groups in London and Moscow. The Beneš faction had lukewarm Allied support. The Czechoslovaks in Moscow, led by Klement Gottwald, the secretary-general of the Czechoslovak Communist party, enjoyed total Soviet backing. Czechoslovak forces fought both on the side of the Allies in the west and as part of Soviet armies in the east. But it was the degree of support given the two Czechoslovak factions that in the end determined the fate of the unhappy country.

As the Soviet forces from the east and the American armies from the west converged on Prague in the closing days of the war, Beneš went to Moscow to negotiate with the Czech and Slovak Communists for the establishment of a national government. On April 4, 1945, they agreed on a National Unity government with the aging Beneš as president. Jan Masaryk, the son of the late founder of the Czechoslovak Republic, came from London to be confirmed as foreign minister. In fact, Beneš seemed to have done quite well. Thirteen cabinet seats went to non-Communists and only seven to Communists.

Beneš's apparent success was an illusion, as the country was to find out before too long. The defense minister, for example, was to be a "nonpartisan" figure. He turned out, however, to be Ludvík Svoboda, a Czech Communist general who had won the title "Hero of the Soviet Union." He was to play a number of contradictory roles in the years to come. The premier was Zdeněk Fierlinger, a pro-Soviet Marxist Social Democrat. Two of the four deputy premiers were Communists. The all-important Interior Ministry, which controlled the police, was given to the Communists along with the equally strategic ministries of Information and Culture, Education, and Social Welfare.

The new government came into being on April 5, under Soviet auspices in the Slovak town of Košice, which recently had been liberated by the Russians. There, Beneš and his ministers awaited the liberation of Prague.

Prague was taken on May 9, 1945, by Soviet troops. United States forces had not liberated the city first because of complex political reasons arising from the wartime alliance with Moscow. Actually, General George S. Patton's Third Army had reached Plzeň (Pilsen) on May 5, and his tanks were ready to roll on to Prague, less than two hours away, at a moment's notice. German resistance had melted away except for one division in Prague that tried in a halfhearted fashion to put down an uprising by Communist-led Czech patriots. Soviet armies were still four days away from the capital. But Patton, who had already sent advance liaison officers to Prague, was ordered to remain in place despite frantic appeals to President Harry Truman by Britain's prime minister, Winston Churchill. The British felt that on his return to Prague, President Beneš would need the moral support offered by the presence of American forces to cope with the anticipated Communist pressures. It is quite possible that the postwar history of Eastern Europe would have developed differently if Patton had been permitted to take Prague.

As it happened, Beneš was allowed to remain in office—and Czechoslovakia to live as a democracy—for just under three years. This period was one of a mounting struggle between the Communist party, which was determined to capture total power in the country, and the Beneš democrats striving to survive. There were outside pressures, too. Czechoslovakia tried to join the Marshall Plan in 1947 to participate in the United States program for Europe's reconstruction. Moscow

Munich, September 29, 1938. The participants in the Munich Agreement were (left to right) Neville Chamberlain, Edouard Daladier, Adolf Hitler, and Benito Mussolini.

The last official photograph of Eduard Beneš, the president of Czechoslovakia until it became one of the Communist-bloc nations in 1948.

vetoed the action on the grounds that it would be a hostile move toward the Soviet Union.

At home, the Communists gradually tightened the noose around the neck of the Beneš regime. The party had polled only 38 percent of the popular vote in the 1946 parliamentary elections. Its own calculations were that it would do even worse in the 1948 elections. The alternative was direct action. Preparations began for the complete overthrow of the Beneš government. Communist revolutionary action committees were established throughout the country. On February 13, 1948, Parliament was told that a "plot" against the republic was afoot. The police were completely dominated by Communists and the partly reactivated its armed people's militia. Suddenly, the country faced a major crisis.

On February 19, the Soviet deputy foreign minister Valerian A. Zorin, arrived in Prague to warn Beneš's ministers that Moscow would not tolerate their ties with "foreign reactionary governments." He said that "the Soviet Union might be forced to safeguard Czechoslovakia's independence." These words were uttered again twenty years later and echoed the past, too. As Beneš said, it was "Munich all over again."

On February 25, President Beneš accepted a new cabinet submitted to him by Gottwald, the head of the Communist party. Beneš had been forced to give in to the threats of Soviet intervention and the knowledge that General Svoboda, the "nonpartisan" defense minister, would not defend the government. Two days later, Beneš left for his country home. He was never again to return to Prague. On March 10, Jan Masaryk, the foreign minister, was found dead in the courtyard of his ministry, the victim of a fall from the window of his office.

This was the end of the Czechoslovak democracy and the beginning of a long nightmare of terror and oppression.

The Nightmare

In 1948, with the disappearance of the Beneš regime in Czechoslovakia, the Soviet Union established its total political and ideological control over Eastern Europe. In previous years, Moscow had gradually implanted Communist rule in East Germany, Bulgaria, Rumania, Hungary, and Poland. Yugoslavia and Albania also had Communist regimes though, as it turned out, they were soon to defy the Russians.

In Czechoslovakia, which had become a "People's Democracy" after the February 25 coup, the immediate concern of the victorious Communists was to consolidate their power. People's courts were established to deal with " counterrevolutionaries." Most industry and commerce were nationalized. The party launched a frantic membership drive. It increased its numbers from slightly over one million before the coup to two and one-half million in November, 1948–18 percent of the total population. Following Beneš's formal resignation from the presidency in June, Klement Gottwald moved into Hradčany Castle to become Czechoslovakia's first Communist president. Antonín Zápotocký, another party old-timer, was named premier, and Rudolf Slánský took over as general secretary of the party.

But no sooner was the Moscow-directed rule established in Czechoslovakia than the whole newly built Communist structure in Eastern Europe was shaken by Yugoslavia's break with the Soviet Union. In 1948, the mounting quarrel between Tito and Stalin, the Soviet leader, resulted in Yugoslavia's expulsion from the Cominform, the now defunct organization of European Communist states. This development was to have far-reaching consequences in Czechoslovakia, as it did elsewhere in the region. This was the first of the many times that nationalism clashed with the Soviet ideal of a unified Communist world directed by Moscow. Inevitably, the Russians moved on all fronts to isolate and nip in the bud this new threat.

"Titoism" became a dirty word in Eastern Europe. It was used by Moscow–along with charges of "Trotskyism" (allegiance to Leon

Soviet Marshal Nikolai Bulganin (left) and President Klement Gottwald at the fourth anniversary celebration of the liberation of Czechoslovakia by Soviet troops in 1945.

Trotsky, an early Soviet leader who had been expelled in the 1920s), Zionism, treason, espionage, and links with the Gestapo and Western intelligence agencies–to hurl against all those suspected of nationalism. Moscow believed in preventive liquidation.

In Poland, where the first anti-Titoist purge took place, the principal victim was the Communist party's leader, Władysław Gomułka, who was fired in the summer of 1948. The following year, a Soviet army marshal was made Poland's defense minister. Gomułka was imprisoned and widespread purges continued into the early 1950s.

In Bulgaria the leading victim of the anti-Titoist purge was Traicho Kostov, the political secretary of the Communist party and acting premier. He was executed in 1949, while scores of ministers and generals were imprisoned. Then, the purges moved to Hungary where László Rajk, the interior minister, was arrested on "Titoist" and "anti-Soviet" charges. A major show trial was held in the capital city, Budapest, leading to the execution of Rajk and two senior military officers. Rajk was linked, among other things, with the United States Central Intelligence Agency and with groups of foreign veterans who had served on the Republican side in the Spanish Civil War ten years earlier. In 1950 and 1951, Hungarian Communists were struck by two more large-scale purges. The 1951 purge resulted in the imprisonment of interior minister János Kadár, a man who was to play a crucial role in subsequent Hungarian history.

Late in 1949, the Soviet campaign against real or imagined "Titoism" shifted from Hungary to Czechoslovakia. For five years, a savage purge swept the country. In Communist history it was comparable only to the great Soviet purges of the 1930s and those in China in the 1950s and 1960s. In the process, a whole Communist generation was destroyed. Eleven top party and government leaders, including Slánský, the party boss, were executed. There were tens of thousands of arrests–the exact number remains unknown–and hundreds of thousands were dismissed from jobs. Trials were held against "Titoists," "Zionists," clergymen of all religions, and just about anyone whom the Czechoslovak and Soviet security forces, working hand in hand, chose to accuse of being "enemies" of the people.

Even when Czechoslovak Communist historians were free to investigate in 1968, they were unable to explain clearly what had prompted a purge of such scope, intensity, and length. There is no real evidence to suggest that a massive conspiracy really was afoot in Czechoslovakia, involving men and women in the highest ranks of the Communist party and government. Looking back, no reason for such a conspiracy can be detected.

What seems to have happened is that the Soviet fear of "Titoism," or nationalism, prompted the Kremlin and its closest associates in Czechoslovakia to launch a political housecleaning of such proportions as to discourage anyone from ever *thinking* about Titoism—let alone practicing it. Indeed, the prosecutor in the Slánský trial told the court that in sentencing its top leaders to death and prison, Czechoslovakia was acting against the same "band of traitors" who had already been punished in the other Eastern European countries. A common theme in all these situations—one that first emerged in 1948 to justify the Communist coup and again in 1968 to justify the Soviet invasion—was the emphasis on Moscow's role in "saving" Czechoslovakia. Put another way, of course, this meant that Moscow repeatedly felt the need to adopt drastic methods to assure itself of total domination in Eastern Europe.

But history has proved, over and over again, that repression does not guarantee the kind of acceptance and support from the people that the Russians were seeking from the Czechs, the Slovaks, and the other Eastern Europeans. In fact, repression tends to become self-defeating in the long run.

In the case of Czechoslovakia, there is no doubt that the purges and the trials of the early 1950s—the whole atmosphere of terror surrounding the nation's life for nearly five years—planted the seeds of the liberal rebellion in 1968. The facts show that the hard core of the progressive Communist leadership in 1968 was made up mainly of men who had spent years in prison as a result of the Great Purge.

General Svoboda, later president, was among these prisoners, as were General Josef Pavel, the interior minister in 1968, Josef Smrkovský, the chairman of Parliament in 1968, and many others. Curiously, one of the ex-prisoners, sentenced to a life term, was Gustav Husák, the Slovak Communist leader. Husák first played a major role in the 1968 rebellion, then made an about-face to take over the country after the Soviet invasion and the removal of Alexander Dubček from office. Just as strangely, Dubček himself, an obscure Communist functionary in Slovakia in the 1950s, was untouched by the purges and left free to pursue his political career—which culminated in 1968.

Reactions to the terror began developing almost immediately on many levels and in a variety of ways. As early as June 1, 1953, a major workers' rebellion erupted in the industrial city of Plzeň, in western Czechoslovakia. It was a protest against both the tensions generated by the purges and a sudden currency reform. Soviet and Communist party flags were burned. It took army troops, supported by tanks and artillery, to quell the riots.

The official response in Czechoslovakia to the events of Plzeň, and other stirrings among the population, took the form of new arrests and trials. But times were changing. Stalin had died in Moscow earlier in the year. President Gottwald was also dead. A sense of relief—and even hope—was evident throughout the whole region. Czechoslovakia's new president was Antonín Zápotocký, the rather popular man who had served as premier. The new first secretary was Antonín Novotný, a loyal party member who was fated to preside over the transition to the Prague Spring.

This transition was slow in coming, but once begun it was irreversible. General Svoboda, for instance, was unexpectedly named to the ruling body of Parliament only a year after Stalin had ordered his release from prison. By mid-1954, Soviet security advisers had left Czechoslovakia. About the same time, the party and the government quietly began to review some of the sentences resulting from the purge trials. Conditions in the prisons suddenly improved.

Antonín Novotný, first secretary of the Communist party and later also president of the Czechoslovak Socialist Republic, who presided over the transition to the Prague Spring.

For one thing, the situation in the whole Communist world was changing. Nikita Khrushchev, the new Soviet leader, made peace with Tito's Yugoslavia and the fantasy of the "Titoist" conspiracies began to crumble. By 1955, the Hungarian government had rehabilitated László Rajk. Between the end of 1955 and the start of 1956, some of the key Czechoslovak prisoners gained their freedom. Among them were Smrkovský, Pavel, and most of the codefendants in the Slánský trial.

Then came the great turning point in Communist history: Khrushchev's "secret speech" before the Twentieth Congress of the Soviet Communist party on the night of February 24–25, 1956. In his speech, Khrushchev indicted Stalin for his "mass repressions," his "persecution mania," and his purges and trials.

The Khrushchev speech provided the signal progressive Communists and others in Eastern Europe needed to set in motion the long-awaited wave of liberalism and reform. Rebellions against orthodox Communism erupted in Poland and Hungary. There is no question that one root of the Czechoslovak experiment of 1968 is to be found in Khrushchev's demolition of the Stalin myth and his observation that there are "different roads to Socialism."

As early as April, 1956, the Czechoslovak Communist party was busy backtracking on the excesses of the early 1950s. It fired Alexei Čepička, the deputy premier and defense minister, who had played a major part in the great purges. The party watched quietly as rebellion grew among Czechoslovakia's intellectuals.

This rebellion started among the writers and journalists, then spread to the moviemakers, who launched the great period in Czechoslovak cinematic arts. The new novels and poems ignored all the official taboos on literature, speaking out frankly on all the subjects. Magazines defied censorship in criticizing the state of affairs in the country.

Next door, in Poland, intellectuals were also rebelling. Suddenly, the Polish Communist party astounded the nation by ousting its hard-line leaders. And some thirty thousand people were freed from prisons, including key party members who had been imprisoned for nearly eight years. Similar events took place in Hungary on the other side of Czechoslovakia.

During the summer of 1956 the ferment in Poland and Hungary reached fever pitch. By October, Gomułka, who had been imprisoned in 1951, was named first secretary of the Communist party. Events were moving so rapidly that Khrushchev flew to Warsaw for a showdown with the new Polish leadership at the same time that Soviet armored units moved on the capital. A clash was averted through a compromise. The Russians recognized the Polish "road to Socialism" and Gomułka assured them he would not leave the Soviet bloc.

In Hungary, conflict could not be avoided. The party leadership was overthrown and Imre Nagy, a progressive Communist, was returned to the premiership he had held earlier. Hungarian students and army troops fought Soviet tanks and infantry in the streets of Budapest. On October 29, Nagy formally proclaimed the end of the Communist party's rule. He formed a coalition government, demanded the departure of all Soviet troops from Hungary, and announced that the country was quitting the Warsaw Pact to become fully neutral.

This was too much for Moscow. On November 4, Soviet tanks invaded Budapest and put an end to the Hungarian rebellion. Nagy was taken to the Soviet Union and executed. János Kadár, who had been imprisoned during the purges, emerged as Hungary's top leader.

The suppression of the Hungarian revolution in 1956 forced Czechoslovakia's rebel intellectuals to become more careful. For the next four years, Czechoslovak Communist liberals had to keep their ideas pretty much to themselves. But people knew that it was only a question of time before the reform movement would be set in motion again.

The year 1960 marked the elevation of Czechoslovakia from a people's democracy to the status of a "Socialist Republic." To celebrate, there was an amnesty under which additional thousands were released from prisons–including Gustav Husák. That same year,

Alexander Dubček, then thirty-nine years old, reached political eminence. He was given the important post of member of the Secretariat of the Central Committee of the Communist party. Another man who was to become well known in 1968 was Oldřich Černík, who joined the Secretariat at the same time as Dubček.

During the next seven years, there was a slow movement toward liberalization. The process was full of ups and downs. But the direction was clear. Writers, journalists, and movie-makers were again in the forefront of reform. An economic crisis forced the party to give considerable power to liberal young economists such as Ota Šik. In 1963, a party commission presented a report that essentially declared that the purges of the previous decade had been a sham. Additional hard-line party leaders were dismissed. Throughout this period Dubček acted most inconspicuously. In fact, few people ever thought of him as the leader of the approaching great rebellion.

The Night Ends

The great rebellion–the Prague Spring of 1968–actually began taking shape in the opening months of 1967 when Czechoslovakia was caught in a series of domestic and international crises.

Antonín Novotný, now serving as both president of Czechoslovakia and first secretary of the Communist party, was ruling over a rapidly crumbling political system. The country, which was trying to improve its economy and social standards in the face of out-of-date laws and procedures inherited from the Stalinist era, was restless. The Communist party was split increasingly between the old-line leadership, as represented by Novotný and his immediate associates, and the younger Communist generation with its fresh ideas about the running of a Socialist state.

The event that touched off the final crisis, which grew into the rebellion, was the Six-Day Arab-Israeli war of June, 1967. The Soviet

Union, followed by all its allies except Rumania, sided with the Arabs and broke off diplomatic relations with Israel. On June 9, 1967, the Novotný regime followed Moscow's lead and immediately brought the crisis upon itself.

Condemnation of Israel was equated by Czechoslovaks with anti-Semitism. This, in turn, was associated in their minds with Stalinism and the trials of the 1950s when "anti-Zionism" and anti-Semitism played a major role in the great purge. Many purge victims, such as the Communist party's boss, Slánský, were Jewish. Unlike its Eastern European neighbors, Czechoslovakia was relatively free of anti-Semitic prejudice. For younger Czechoslovaks, there even was the parallel between Israel's lone stand in the Arab world and their own country's growing isolation in the midst of orthodox Communism.

The controversy came to a head at the Fourth Congress of the Writers' Union in Prague between June 27 and 29. It was the first time a writers' congress had been held since 1963. As it developed, it was the turning point in the rising campaign of the intellectuals against Novotný. The congress set in motion the forces that were to produce the Prague Spring. Pavel Kohout, a well-known playwright, touched off the battle with a speech denouncing the anti-Israel policy. He was followed by Jan Proházka, one of the country's leading writers, and the novelists Milan Kundera and Ludvík Vaculík, all demanding cultural freedom. Then, Ladislav Mňačko, Czechoslovakia's top novelist, simply left for Israel with a ringing proclamation that "the system in Czechoslovakia must be changed to a very considerable degree if we want to continue as a healthy socialist humanitarian country."

Novotný was now on the defensive, although the regime forbade the publication of the speeches delivered at the congress. President Novotný himself said in a later address that "we certainly cannot tolerate accusations that in the past we have been passing through a 'second dark age.' " In September, after a visit to the Soviet Union,

Hradčany Castle—the seat of Czechoslovakia's governments for about a thousand years—and St. Vitus Cathedral soar above the capital city, Prague.

Novotný significantly warned that "liberalism" was spreading in Czechoslovakia and that it was imperative to "come out openly against this phenomenon." Soon after, the most outspoken of the writers at the June congress were expelled from the Communist party. *Literárni Noviny* (*Literary News*), the Writers' Union's magazine, was taken over by the Culture and Information Ministry, which promptly fired all the editors. In December, 1967, the regime restricted foreign travel by Czechoslovaks.

It may have seemed that Novotný had ended the intellectuals' revolt and survived their challenge to his rule. But, in fact, the real crisis was now at hand. It was not only the intellectuals who were preparing a counteroffensive which, perhaps, was a relatively minor element in the situation. More menacingly, the national economy was collapsing. And, at the same time, the nationalist-minded Slovaks were set to blast Novotný out of power. In past months, Novotný had managed to go out of his way to insult the Slovaks and their cultural heritage.

Although since early 1967 Novotný had allowed the party's young economists to experiment with economic reform ideas, he had kept them from putting them in practice. Prices rose rapidly. Production dropped because the workers were uninterested and sometimes simply did not come to work. The famous Czech industrial quality standards hit bottom. Housing programs were paralyzed. By September, all this was translated into active political opposition to Novotný.

At a September meeting of the party's Central Committee, Alexander Dubček, the new Presidium member from Slovakia and chief of the Slovak branch of the party, rose to protest the failures of the government's economic policy. He complained that Slovakia's share of the national investment was running well below what Prague had promised. He made it clear that, in general, the Slovaks considered themselves ill-treated by the Prague-based Novotný government. From that day on, Dubček began to emerge as an opposition leader within the Politburo. He was more than a Slovak spokesman because many of his criticisms also were directed at the regime's oppressive handling of intellectuals in Czech and Slovak lands alike. Novotný's unspoken response was to have Dubček followed by the secret police.

At the October 30 meeting of the party, Dubček accused Novotný of "behaving like a dictator." Dubček said Novotný had deliberately sabotaged economic reforms and harmfully interfered with the Slovak economy. In a wild exchange of threats with Novotný, Dubček demanded political reform in the country "starting at the top, with the party leadership." Novotný countered with the charge that Dubček was a "bourgeois nationalist," as grave an accusation as can be made in a Communist country. On November 1, members of the Central Committee began urging Novotný to resign as the party's first secretary. Novotný reacted by adjourning the meeting.

But that same evening a full-fledged riot erupted at Prague University. The students presumably were protesting against the conditions in their dormitories, but the demonstration was clearly political in character. When they tried to march on Hradčany Castle, the police chased them back to the campus with tear gas and clubs. There was a lot of police brutality involved in quelling the riot. This, too, became an ingredient of the gathering crisis.

The month of November was marked by widespread protests against police behavior in the student riot. Within the Communist party the opposition to Novotný was growing in strength. As the December snow whitened Prague, Novotný had his back to the wall.

But he and his Soviet allies fought to reverse the course of events. On December 4 the army announced that major military maneuvers were being held in Bohemia. Since winter war games are highly unusual in normal circumstances, it looked as if Novotný had called out the troops to encircle Prague, which would assure his hold on power.

On December 9 the Soviet Communist party general secretary, Leonid I. Brezhnev, arrived in Prague–reportedly on the recommendation of his ambassador in the Czechoslovak capital. Brezhnev met with the full Presidium of the Czechoslovak party, except for Dubček, to measure the situation. Then he rose to his feet and said he was returning to Moscow. His parting comment was that the Novotný crisis was "your Czechoslovak affair" and that "the Soviet party and the Soviet Union will not interfere in your internal affairs." It was a remark that was to haunt Brezhnev in the coming months. On his way home, Brezhnev stopped off in Bratislava to confer with Dubček, who then still seemed to be the loyal follower of Moscow that he had always been.

Left to his own devices and facing the threat of being ousted, Novotný now moved to do away with his opponents. He planned to bring troops into Prague on December 16, the day when the party's Central Committee was to meet again–presumably to remove Novotný from power. Because the army required a few extra days to make the move, Novotný postponed the party meeting. But orders were drawn up for the arrests of all the progressive Communist leaders. A general who opposed Novotný's move informed Dubček and his associates of the conspiracy.

On December 18, a secret emergency meeting of the party Presidium was held. Novotný was faced with documentary proof of his attempt to destroy his opposition. He denied it, but within hours orders went out to the army to suspend the maneuvers. The overthrow of Novotný's enemies–and, possibly, a civil war–was avoided by a matter of hours. The full Central Committee of the party was called into session at the same time as the permanent session of the Presidium. Novotný knew his days were numbered.

For the next three days, Novotný fought his tormentors to a standoff. Dubček and his allies could not muster the votes in the Presidium to oust Novotný, chiefly because there was no agreement on his successor as the party's first secretary. The battle was then adjourned until after the Christmas and New Year holidays. The outside world, and even most Czechoslovaks, were hardly aware that a historic power struggle was under way.

The Presidium and the Central Committee met again on January 2, 1968. This time, the progressive group had the votes to bring Novotný down. Late in the evening of January 4, the final vote in the Presidium was taken. Novotný was no longer the party's first secretary.

However, the Presidium ruled that the party's top post and the presidency of the republic henceforth would be separated. As a result, Novotný was allowed to keep the title of President of Czechoslovakia, but no power went with it. Dubček's own election as the new first secretary came at dawn on January 5.

"A Year is Eight Months," a leading Czechoslovak journalist wrote after the events of 1968. The eight months of the Prague Spring were the period between Dubček's rise to power in January and the entry of Soviet troops in Prague in August. But even this short period was divided into two distinct segments. From January until April, Czechoslovak Communists searched for a definition of their revolution. During the months after April, the revolution acquired its full identity as "Marxism with a Human Face."

It is important to remember two things about these events. The first is that when Alexander Dubček assumed the direction of the Czechoslovak Communist party, he may not have suspected that history was to cast him in the role of leading one of the most important schisms in Communist history.

Second, lack of public interest in Novotný's fall was due largely to Czechoslovaks' cynicism about leadership changes and a total lack of obvious drama accompanying the changeover. There were no stirring proclamations and no savage attacks on the deposed leaders. There were no purges, which in the past were always associated with violent changes in the party leadership. Aside from a tiny group of insiders who understood the meaning of the January 5 events, the population could not be blamed for thinking that this was just another tiresome game of Communist musical chairs.

The Prague Spring

From January to March 1968, politics seemed unchanged. Novotný was still the president. Dubček added four new members to the Presidium, two progressives and two conservatives: the political balance of power thus was preserved. However, one of the new Presidium members was Josef Špaček, the fiercely progressive first secretary of one of the party's major districts.

But Dubček kept to himself. He made no speeches. He even discouraged party newspapers from filling their pages with the usual praise due a first secretary. A modest man, he appeared content to keep things as they were, except for a change here or there, and to try to improve the functioning of the country and its economy.

One of the mysteries of the Prague Spring, of course, is how Dubček turned into the standard-bearer of Communist liberalism. One believable theory is based on conversations with several of Dubček's close friends. It is that after taking office as first secretary, he discovered in the party files the gory details of the persecutions, brutalities, and injustices of the past twenty years. It was said that Dubček wept when he read these documents and vowed that this would never happen again under Communism in Czechoslovakia.

In addition, powerful new pressures were centering on Dubček. At the beginning, they came from two men who, in different ways, were to be closely associated with Czechoslovakia's later history.

One was Gustav Husák, the Slovak Communist intellectual, once sentenced to a life term in prison. As early as January 12 Husák wrote in an article in a Bratislava magazine that "we need today the activity and engagement of all who have at heart the progressive solution of our problems, the modernization of our society, and the completion of the revival process of socialist theory and practice. . . . We can only hope that the year 1968 has moved our society on to a new phase of development." Three weeks later, Husák stated in another article that reforms were slow in coming and that people were watching the new situation with hope but also with "old skepticism." This was the man who less than a year later was to ally himself with Moscow against Dubček's progressive rebellion.

The other powerful influence on Dubček came from Josef Smrkovský. He was the man who had led the anti-Nazi uprising in Prague in 1945, spent years in prison during the purges, then returned to prominence as a member of the party's Central Committee and a cabinet minister under Novotný. Writing during January Smrkovoský said that "we must determinedly correct, repair, and rectify the deformations of Socialism which occurred in the past, and we must not permit new ones to arise."

As January turned into February, a new mood was developing in Czechoslovakia. Špaček, the new Presidium member, was busily sending emissaries to regional party organizations to inform them that repression was over and fresh ideas were welcomed from anyone. And, inevitably, the intellectuals moved to assert themselves as the leaders of the new movement.

The Writers' Union, which had been smashed by Novotný only a few months earlier, met late in January to elect progressive leaders—this time without interference from the party's cultural censors. The union again took over its magazine, which was destined to be the voice of the Prague Spring.

Perhaps all of this should have alarmed Moscow, but it seems the Kremlin was not yet taking the Czechoslovak experiment seriously. Dubček had flown to Moscow on January 29 for friendly meetings with the Soviet leaders. Brezhnev offered him his warm congratulations. Then Dubček held the customary meetings with his Communist neighbors: Hungary's Kadár and Poland's Gomułka. If Dubček already had "subversive" ideas about Czechoslovakia's course in its relations with the other Communist powers, he obviously kept them to himself. For the time being, Moscow and its allies felt secure about the Dubček leadership.

But it soon became clear that they had underestimated the feelings of the Czechs, whose struggle for independence dated back to the time of John Huss. They had also underestimated the importance of the new generation of Communist philosophers and writers whose sympathies were with the West. The Russians never understood what was happening more and more quickly in Prague.

In February, for example, Czechoslovak writers and journalists won the party's agreement that press censorship simply should be

DŮSLEDNÉ POKRAČOVÁNÍ V POLEDNOVÉ
ZÁKLADEM JEDNOTY SPOLEČNOSTI

abolished. Actually, the party had no power to repeal the existing press law. It just let press freedom happen. Such a thing had never happened before in a Communist country and now the floodgates were open.

On February 1 Dubček, speaking to an audience of farmers, took his first major public step in the direction of reforming the Czechoslovak society. He announced that the party was drafting an "Action Program" that would spell out the aims of the "new Socialist society." It was to be the principal political document of the Prague Spring. Dubček modestly told his audience that "democracy is not only the right and chance to pronounce one's own views, but also the way in which people's views are handled: whether they have a real feeling of coresponsibility, codecision, whether they really feel they are participating in making decisions and solving important problems."

This, too, was a novelty in a Communist state. But the new leadership quickly moved beyond speechmaking. On February 6, the party's Presidium discussed the liberal "Action Program." It then informed the country that henceforth "meetings of the Central Committee should be held in an atmosphere that would enable *"free criticism and creative exchange of views.*" In another radical step, the Presidium pledged that "information about the discussions of the Central Committee and its Secretariat will be published." This marked the end of traditional secrecy and represented the nearest thing to the establishment of functioning democracy within Communism.

The next step in the quickening evolution of Czechoslovak politics had to be an effort to break away from Soviet domination and control. Smrkovský, writing in the party newspaper *Rudé Právo* late in February, put it this way: "It is incumbent on us, on Czechs and on

The growing feedom of the press during the Prague Spring made stopping to read the newspaper an interesting and important part of the day.

Josef Smrkovský addressing workers at a plant in northern Bohemia. The sign says, "Consistent continuation of the post-January politics is the basis for the unity of our society."

Slovaks, to enter courageously into unexplored terrain and in it to look for our Czechoslovak Socialist road." In a radio commentary the same week, Eugen Loebl, an economist who had spent eleven years in prison, asked how long it would take Czechoslovakia to adjust its "unequal relations with the Soviet Union" in the economic realm. Put simply, these unequal relations meant that the Soviet Union had first call on all Czechoslovakia's raw materials from coal to uranium ore. The raw materials were paid for in food, oil, or Soviet currency, which could not be used to make purchases in the West. Because of Czechoslovakia's advanced industry, Moscow also had first call on its industrial products. This left the Czechs no freedom to find other and better markets. It was Moscow that determined the prices Czechoslovakia was paid for its exports—and what it had to pay for its imports from the Soviets. In sum, it was Russian guidance that determined how the Czechoslovak economy should develop—a situation that obviously did little to benefit the Czechoslovaks.

And so it went from criticism to criticism as reformers used their newly discovered freedom to question everything that had been taboo until just a few months earlier.

It was also in February that Dubček began to dismantle the secret police apparatus, which was tied more closely to Moscow than to the Czechoslovak government. By then, coolness had developed between him and Moscow—a sign of the tensions that soon were to characterize Czechoslovak-Soviet relations.

At the twentieth anniversary celebrations of the 1948 Communist take-over, Dubček delivered this summary of his views, while Brezhnev sat in the audience in stony silence:

> *For the [Communist] party, to carry through its leading role in the present situation means first and foremost to create the necessary preconditions for the growth of creative initiative, to provide greater scope for confrontation and exchanges of opinion, to make it possible for every Communist to be informed thoroughly, objectively, and in good time about events in his own country and abroad, so that he may possess a point of view with*

regard to the party's policy and, particularly, in framing the party's political policy and in its actions, especially in the sphere in which he is employed.

Meanwhile, the revolutionary process speeded up in all areas of Czechoslovak life. Early in March, the Army General Staff issued a public statement that disclosed Novotný's December attempts to unleash a military coup and demanded his resignation from the presidency. During March, members of the party's Presidium held sixty-seven meetings with district organizations to discuss the "Action Program" and to request the opinions of local leaders. Encouraged by the leadership, party members flooded it with complaints about "mistakes" and "aberrations" of the past. Nothing of the sort had happened in Czechoslovakia since the Communists had taken over twenty years earlier. For the first time since 1948, people were free to express their views—and they did so with enthusiasm.

On March 15, Novotný was forced to fire his interior minister and the prosecutor general, both of whom were involved in the purges of the 1950s. During the same month the Boy Scouts, who had been abolished in 1948 as a "tool of imperialism," were allowed to rebuild their organization. Then the Dubček government lifted the twenty-year-old ban on honoring Tomáš Masaryk, the founder of the First Czechoslovak Republic. Almost instantly, the old president's portraits appeared in store windows and homes. At the same time, the newspapers began asking whether his son, Jan, might not have been murdered by Soviet agents in 1948. On March 20, Smrkovský told a Prague youth rally that "you have the right and the duty to be more radical and more revolutionary." The liberal wave was cresting.

On March 28, Dubček summoned the party's Presidium and Central Committee for a special session. But before they could meet, Novotný submitted his resignation as president. Two days later, the National Assembly elected the seventy-two-year-old General Svoboda as Czechoslovakia's new president. It so happens that *svoboda* in Czech means "freedom," and the nation took it as a good omen. Novotný's departure and Svoboda's election confirmed that the country truly had entered a new era. But the Czechoslovaks did not realize how short-lived that era was to be.

On April 1, Dubček asked the party's Central Committee for approval of the "Action Program." He told his colleagues that the party should not be afraid of the "new wave," but should "learn from it." And, as he put it, the party must defend its policies through persuasion and not force: "Authority must be renewed. . . . It is never given to anyone once and for all."

The heart of the "Action Program" was that the country should enjoy a reasonably free political life under Communist guidance, that it should be given a real economic reform, and that all the victims of the Stalinist purges should be rehabilitated.

The program was approved on April 5, and Dubček again reorganized the party's Presidium. But the pressures from the Soviet Union and domestic Communist conservatives had already grown to such a point that the new leadership turned out to be a deadly compromise. The eleven-man Presidium was split right down the middle between progressives and conservatives. Dubček held the deciding vote. In the coming months, his task was to keep the party together and see to it that the liberal revolution would not get out of hand. It was an impossible job.

The approval of the "Action Program" called for a new government to breathe life into the reforms the party had in mind. Thus on April 8, President Svoboda named Oldřich Černík as premier. Among the five deputy premiers, he gave posts to the liberal economist Ota Šik, the Slovak intellectual Gustav Husák, and the very conservative Lubomir Strougal who had been Novotný's interior min-

When the ban on mentioning Tomáš Masaryk, founder of the first Czechoslovak Republic, was lifted in 1968, stores suddenly blossomed with portraits of him and books describing his life and work.

Dubček was welcomed warmly wherever he went in Czechoslovakia during the Prague Spring.

ister. The cabinet, like the party Presidium, pitted progressives against conservatives.

The problem facing Dubček was that a political rebellion had already been set in motion throughout the country. He was powerless to act as the moderator he had hoped to be. The situation was increasingly out of control and Dubček was being carried along by it. He was in the impossible position of having encouraged a rebellion and then having to keep it from going too far too fast. As a lifelong Communist, Dubček was painfully aware of the limits of Soviet tolerance of the experiment over which he was presiding.

As early as March, Dubček was summoned to a meeting in Dresden, East Germany, with Brezhnev and the other Eastern European leaders to be read the riot act about the consequences of letting Czechoslovakia slip out of the Communist camp. But events were overtaking Dubček. At the same time, Moscow seems to have realized that sooner or later it would have to intervene. As early as April, the party's conservative leaders were plotting with the Soviet embassy in Prague. The Soviet High Command activated plans for an invasion.

Blind to Dubček's concerns, the Czechoslovaks were basking in their new freedoms. Every act of defiance led to another one. An association of former political prisoners made itself into an informal *non*-Communist political party. This was hateful to Moscow. Czech newspapers, including *Rudé Právo,* printed articles denouncing the role of the Soviet secret police in the purges of the 1950s. In effect, the secret police were accused of murdering Jan Masaryk. The Justice Ministry ordered an investigation into the circumstances of his death. A number of officials connected with the purges committed suicide rather than risk exposure. Then the party Presidium ordered Premier Černík to recommend measures for "bilaterally advantageous economic cooperation between Czechoslovakia and the Soviet Union." This was another way of saying that Moscow could no longer depend on its supply of Czechoslovak manufactured goods in exchange for ruble credits that could not be used in international transactions. Finally, Smrkovský, the most outspoken of the progressives, was named chairman of the National Assembly, the parliament that no longer wished to be a rubber stamp for party orders.

May Day came as a symbol of the new Czechoslovakia. Traditionally this holiday honors workers in the Communist countries and is a major annual event. But instead of the usual well-orchestrated Communist celebrations, the 1968 May Day was a happy and good-natured holiday in Czechoslovakia. Dubček, his blue eyes twinkling, was engulfed by a crowd of admirers on Prague's Old Town Square where he gathered kisses and flowers from the young and the old, and dispensed autographs. President Svoboda posthumously awarded the Republic's highest decorations to the principal victims of the purges.

Two days later, the country learned that the Soviet Union insisted on holding Warsaw Pact military maneuvers in Czechoslovakia. To the Czechoslovaks, this meant that the Russians were preparing to invade. A bitter anti-Soviet demonstration took place in Prague. At midnight, Dubček and his key associates suddenly flew to Moscow. They returned within thirty-six hours. Ominously, Dubček told newsmen that "our Soviet friends received with understanding our explanation of our endeavors aimed at the further development of Socialist democracy and at the strengthening of the Communist party as its leading force." Translated into plain language, Dubček had been called on the carpet by the Russians.

By mid-May, Soviet propaganda had pulled out all the stops in denouncing Czechoslovak "provocations." Reports circulated that Warsaw Pact armies were massing on the country's borders. Whether the Russians had planned a strike at Czechoslovakia in May and then changed their minds—or simply wanted to scare the Czechoslovaks—is not known. But from that moment on, the country lived under the threat of an invasion. A "tank psychology" set in.

On May 17, Soviet Premier Aleksei N. Kosygin arrived in Prague, a few hours after the arrival of the defense minister, Marshal Andrei Grechko. He flew back to Moscow after five days of conferences with Czechoslovak leaders. An announcement was made that joint

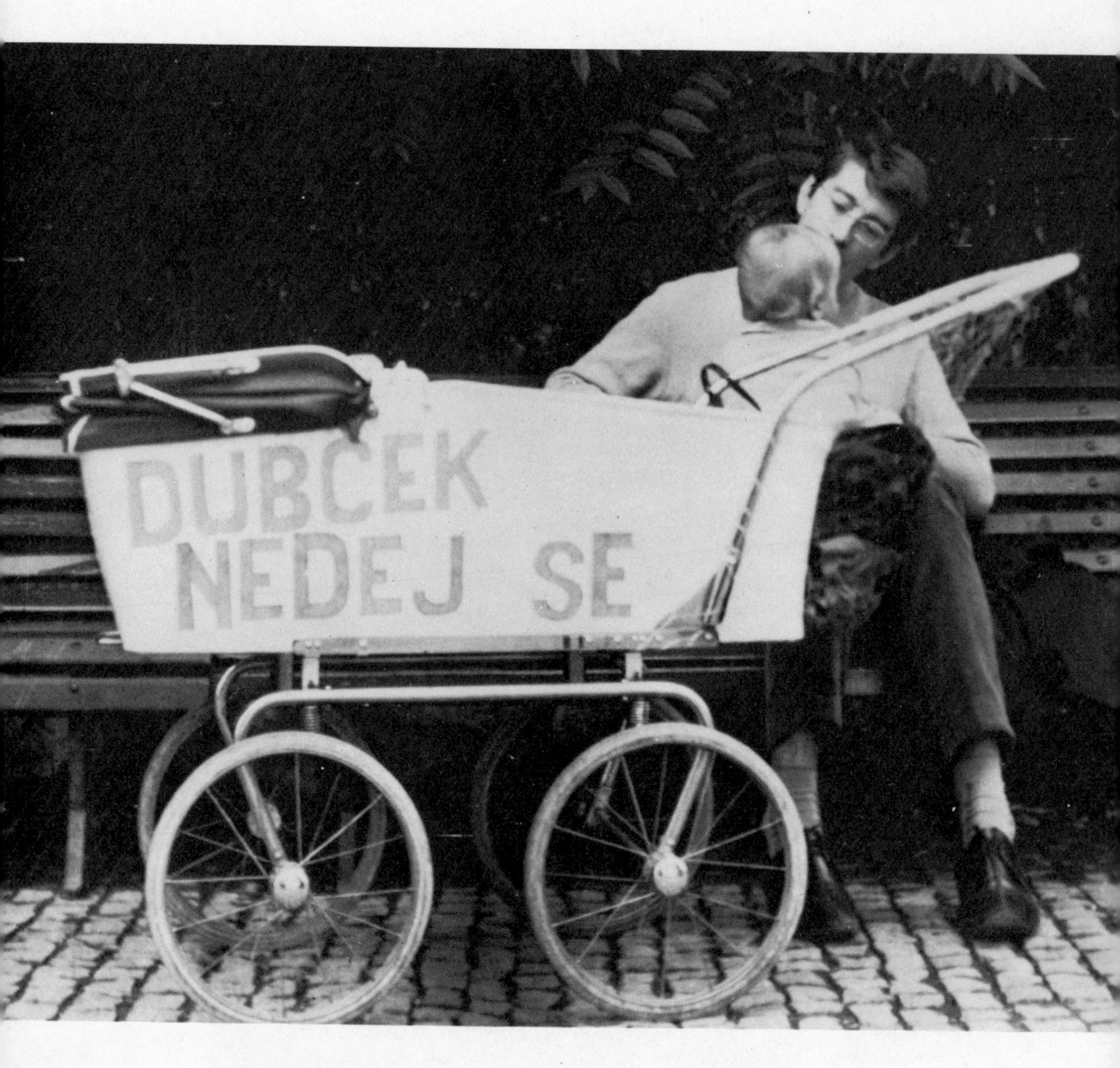

Support for Dubček's policies was expressed in many different ways. This young father painted the words "Dubček, Hold Out! on his son's baby carriage.

"combat readiness" exercises would be held in the country with the participation of Soviet troops. Kosygin's visit may have been the final Soviet attempt to convince Dubček and his colleagues to give up their pursuit of "Marxism with a Human Face."

The Punishment

For the next three months–the remainder of the Prague Spring–relations between Czechoslovakia and the Soviet Union amounted to one continuous confrontation. Moscow's propaganda spoke openly of "counterrevolution" in Czechoslovakia. Prague's intellectuals responded on June 27 with the "Two Thousand Words," an extraordinary document, which warned that "foreign forces may interfere with our internal development" and pledged armed support for the government. Tens of thousands signed the manifesto, which ended with these words: "The spring has just ended and will never return. In the winter we will know everything."

Sixteen thousand Soviet troops, supported by tanks, were on "maneuvers" in Czechoslovakia when the manifesto was published in the Prague newspapers. Even so, Brezhnev immediately telephoned Dubček to protest what he scathingly called the official proclamation of a "counterrevolution." Dubček seems to have interpreted this conversation as an invasion threat. He immediately summoned the party's Presidium into an emergency session. Before long, the Presidium charged that the manifesto was a "clear threat to the entire democratization process." Obviously, Dubček, caught as he was between his progressive friends and the pro-Moscow conservatives, was trying to hit the right note.

But on July 8, Dubček was ordered to attend a meeting in Warsaw with Brezhnev and the other Eastern European leaders to discuss the alleged threat to Communism raised by the manifesto. Dubček refused to go. The meeting, which was held without him, produced a formal communication to Prague on July 16. It stated that "it is our deep conviction that the offensive of the reactionary forces, backed by imperialism, against your party and the foundations of the Socialist system in the Czechoslovak Socialist Republic threatens to push your country off the road of Socialism and thus jeopardize the interests of the entire Socialist system. . . ." Dubček was being warned that an invasion could take place at any time.

On July 23, the Soviets announced that "large-scale" military maneuvers had begun along the Czechoslovak-Ukrainian border, as well as in the western part of the Russian Republic and Byelorussia. But then the Russians unexpectedly proposed a meeting of the top leaderships of the two parties to be held on July 29 in the Czechoslovak border village of Čierna-nad-Tisou.

With Dubček and President Svoboda leading the Czechoslovak group and Brezhnev heading the Soviet delegation, the Čierna conference went on for four days. It produced some kind of agreement, although it was never made public, because Dubček told newsmen on his return to Prague that he had "good news" and that his people could "sleep peacefully."

On August 3, all the Warsaw Pact leaders, including Brezhnev, met in Bratislava with the Czechoslovaks to sign a declaration. It pledged all parties to cooperate on the basis of "equality, sovereignty, national independence, and territorial integrity." Newspaper photographs showed Dubček and Brezhnev kissing each other on the cheeks. Still, nobody was quite certain what the Bratislava Declaration really meant.

But the Czechoslovaks breathed a sigh of relief. It now seemed

Smiles and flowers marked the opening of the Bratislava meeting in August, 1968. Front row (left to right): Ludvík Svoboda, Leonid Brezhnev, Alexander Dubček. Second row (left to right): Aleksei Kosygin, Mikhail Suslov, and Nikolai Podgorny of the U.S.S.R., and Czechoslovak Premier Oldřich Černík.

Young Czechoslovaks gathered around the statue of John Huss in Prague to await word of what had really happened at the Bratislava meeting.

that the danger of an invasion had been ended. Taking advantage of their new freedom to travel abroad, tens of thousands of Czechoslovaks went away on foreign vacations. Nobody realized that Czechoslovakia had only been granted a reprieve of less than three weeks before Warsaw Pact tanks rolled across her borders.

It is not known what, precisely, finally led the Soviet Union to invade Czechoslovakia on the night of August 20. It may be that this decision was taken long before the military move actually was ordered and that the setting of the date was simply a matter of the Warsaw Pact command's convenience in completing troop deployments.

Western and Czechoslovak intelligence officers believe that the Soviet Union began staff planning for the invasion as early as February, about the time that Dubček promised the "Action Program" and began to dismantle the secret police.

To be sure, this invasion was prepared as openly as any in history. Beginning late in April, the Russians made no secret of their troop movements in the vicinity of Czechoslovak frontiers. They seemed, in fact, to advertise them as if to warn Prague that it had better behave. It seems, too, that no country had ever been as thoroughly looked over by the enemy prior to an invasion. Both Defense Minister Grechko and the Warsaw Pact commander-in-chief, Marshal Ivan I. Yakubovsky, were frequent visitors to Prague during the spring of 1968. And, between early June and late July, Soviet troops had been conducting maneuvers inside Czechoslovakia. Actually, the Soviet Union could have announced at any time during the summer that the country was *already* occupied—and simply sent reinforcements.

Naturally, Moscow would have preferred to achieve Dubček's liquidation without an invasion. No matter how well executed, invasions are unpredictable and messy affairs. It would have been more satisfactory for the Russians to avoid paying the political price of armed intervention.

With this in mind, it is highly likely that the Kremlin chose to wait as long as possible, hoping that Prague would put the brakes on its revolution (as Poland had done in 1956) before the situation went entirely out of control. This would explain the succession of Warsaw Pact conferences, the threats, and the propaganda barrage aimed at the Czechoslovak leadership and its "counterrevolution." Finally, it is possible that certain commitments were made to the Russians by Dubček both at Čierna and Bratislava, and that they were not kept. The apparent cordiality of the Bratislava meeting on August 3, made it seem that some kind of basic political agreement had been reached.

But if this was so, nothing in Prague showed that Dubček had the slightest intention of putting the brakes on the rebellion. Instead, he appeared to be speeding it up. In mid-August, Dubček and Svoboda played host at Hradčany Castle first to Yugoslavia's Marshal Tito and then to Rumania's President Nicolae Ceaușescu—the two Communist leaders whose own independence had for years been a thorn in Moscow's flesh. Prague received these visitors with an outpouring of joy that clearly showed the growing anti-Soviet feeling in Czechoslovakia. Diplomats in Prague thought that Czechoslovakia was about to work out a three-part alliance of "independent Communists" with Yugoslavia and Rumania. This, naturally, would have posed a formidable threat to the Soviet hold on Eastern Europe.

On the domestic scene, the Communist party was busily preparing for its Fourteenth Congress, which was scheduled for September. The Congress was to adopt new laws and consolidate the influence of the progressives. In fact, the progressives were known to hope that the Congress, overwhelmingly made up of liberal Communist delegates elected throughout the country during the summer, would finally remove the conservatives from leadership. This would have given Dubček a clear signal to complete his revolution. A preparatory commission published the draft of new party laws that eliminated the sacred Communist principle of "democratic centralism." This meant that even if a decision was taken by a majority, the minority still had the right to express its views in public. Orthodox Communists saw this as a clear threat that the party ultimately would collapse. The proposals also called for open discussions and secret balloting in party forums. This, too, was a potentially mortal blow at the standard practice of Communism.

Moreover, the intellectuals began a campaign to abolish the people's militia, which was traditionally the party's strong-arm organization. In Prague's squares, political discussions were conducted as openly as if they were taking place in London's Hyde Park. To the Russians in Moscow, it must have looked as if Communism was being abolished altogether in Czechoslovakia.

The final phase of the Prague Spring was played out between August 12 and 18. On the 12th, Dubček met in Karlovy Vary with East Germany's Walter Ulbricht. Ulbricht demanded that the Czechoslovaks commit themselves to combating "anti-Socialist forces" and permitting the permanent stationing of Warsaw Pact forces within Czechoslovakia. On the 17th, Dubček met at the border with Hungary's Kadár, who accused him of breaking promises that he allegedly had made at Čierna and Bratislava. On the 18th, the Soviet leadership held a secret meeting at the Kremlin, apparently to approve the invasion. Later that day, Brezhnev dispatched a long letter to Dubček scolding him for betraying the "spirit of Čierna and Bratislava.

Seventy-two hours after sending the letter, Brezhnev ordered the Warsaw Pact armies into Czechoslovakia. The occupation succeeded militarily, but the Russians suddenly found themselves frustrated when it came time to impose their political domination. The Czech resistance spirit soared during what was left of the summer and well into the fall of 1968.

Winter...Again

As autumn turned into winter, the Soviet power gradually asserted itself in Prague. The demonstrations went on. Courageous journalists and intellectuals continued to speak out. But the process of "normalization"—under the watchful eye of Soviet occupation troops—went on. One by one, progressive leaders were removed from their posts, as were editors of newspapers and magazines. Radio and television began to sink into conformity. Svoboda and Dubček still made brave speeches about Czechoslovakia's future, but now caution was the dominant theme. Soviet troops were withdrawn from Prague and deployed in the countryside. But the Czechoslovak leadership daily reminded the people that the troops would return to Prague instantly if "normalization" broke down.

Winter was a sad time in Prague. In January, 1969, a young man named Jan Palach burned himself to death on Wenceslaus Square in protest against the occupation. His funeral was a huge but peaceful patriotic demonstration—as if the people were saying farewell not only to him but to the Prague Spring as well.

April brought another crisis. The Czechoslovak ice hockey team defeated the Soviet team in a world championship game in Stockholm. Crowds celebrating the victory ran through the streets of Prague. They burned the offices of the Soviet airline and attacked Soviet military headquarters. Moscow rushed Marshal Grechko, the defense minister, to Prague to restore order and deliver the final blow to the remnants of the 1968 revolution.

On April 17, the party Presidium met under the threat of a new Soviet move to accept Dubček's resignation from his post as first secretary. The man chosen to replace him was Gustav Husák, once the fervent supporter of the revolution and now the tough spokesman for Soviet interests.

The rest of the story is melancholy. Dubček was permitted a brief stint as ambassador to Turkey. Late in 1969 he was brought home to become a non-person. He was exiled to his native Slovakia. Smrkovský, the fiery National Assembly chairman, seemed to disappear. Before too long, Premier Černík was also dropped. Journalists, editors, professors, writers, and other intellectuals of the Prague Spring were forced to take menial jobs.

It has been argued that in cooperating with the Soviet Union—with seventy thousand Soviet troops permanently stationed in Czechoslovakia under a treaty signed late in 1968—Husák and Svoboda may have saved the country from an even worse fate. It has been said that they wrested from the Russians the promise that none

of the leaders of the Prague Spring would stand public trial—an idea the Kremlin apparently favored as late as 1969.

All this may be true. Perhaps some day history will offer the full account of the postinvasion period. But since 1969, Czechoslovakia has lived silently as one of the most politically backward Communist nations of Europe, even though a major thaw has relaxed the tensions between the East and the West. Years after the invasion, repression of ideas still continued in Czechoslovakia. Scores of minor personalities were tried on a variety of "subversive" charges, but sentenced to relatively short prison terms. These trials served chiefly as a warning to others who might again begin entertaining liberal ideas.

Prevented from having a political voice, Czechoslovakia's people withdrew into themselves. Sports events—soccer in warm weather and ice hockey in the winter—became occasions for total national interest. People watched bad movies, worried about things like jobs, food, and heat in wintertime, and went through all the normal motions of life in a strange pretense that nothing had happened to shake the life of the country during the brief and exciting experiment in 1968.

In the end, the reality was that Czechoslovakia was grievously punished for the Prague Spring.

Historically, the crucial question is whether the Prague Spring was an isolated episode or part of a broader process that is bound to continue with ups and downs across Eastern Europe.

It already seems clear that the Czechoslovak events of 1968 were an integral and dramatic chapter in the history of communism. They

Czechoslovakia's fiftieth anniversary as an independent nation took place in October following the invasion. A quiet celebration was held in the Spanish Hall at the Hradčany featuring speeches by leaders of the Prague Spring as (left to right) Josef Smrkovský, Ludvík Svoboda, Alexander Dubček, Oldřich Černík, Evzen Erban.

Gustav Husák, who succeeded Dubček as first secretary of the Czechoslovak Communist party, addressing a party congress in 1971.

After the Czechoslovak ice hockey team beat the Soviet team 4 to 3 in the spring of 1969, the streets of Prague were again, briefly, filled with happy and rioting people.

were preceded by the Polish and Hungarian uprisings of 1956, and, as it turned out, they were to be followed by new shocks reverberating throughout Eastern Europe.

Thus, Polish workers rebelled once more in 1970, this time over economic issues. They fought pitched battles with the regime's police in what nearly developed into a civil war in northwestern Poland. The spectre of a Soviet intervention rose again. But, perhaps remembering Czechoslovakia's fate, the Polish Communist leadership chose to give into workers' demands.

Władysław Gomułka, once a Communist liberal and, in 1968, a chief proponent of Czechoslovakia's invasion, was ousted from the post of first secretary and replaced by Edward Gierek, a younger and more progressive Communist leader. Gierek has made no attempt to repeat Dubček's performance but, since his advent to power, Poland has enjoyed a surprising amount of freedom. In Communist terms, at least, Polish politics have become participatory and the party has become decentralized. Many of the ideas of the 1968 Prague Spring have found quiet acceptance in Poland, even though the Poles have not considered it necessary to engage in loud talk about it.

In East Germany, Walter Ulbricht, a throwback to Stalinism, quietly was removed from leadership soon after the events of 1970 in Poland. A measure of relaxation developed in East Germany, long one of the most politically repressive Communist states. The 1972 treaty between East and West Germany, which probably would have been impossible in Ulbricht's time, opened an additional channel for the circulation of ideas. Hungary has maintained a steady, quiet policy of relative political liberalization accompanied by a successful economic reform.

It is troublesome to predict history. But if the past is to be a guide, the liberalizing process in Communist Eastern Europe, so brutally interrupted in Czechoslovakia in 1968, must inevitably move ahead. The new generations will see to it.

Chronology

1948 Czechoslovak People's Democracy established.

1949 Purge trials begin in Czechoslovakia to eliminate "enemies" of the state.

1953 Klement Gottwald dies and is replaced in office by Antonín Novotný.

1956 Nikita Khrushchev denounces Stalin in "secret speech."

1960 Czechoslovakia now named a Socialist Republic but its political, cultural, and economic life stagnant.

1967 *June*—Arab-Israeli War begins and anti-Israel moves of Novotný government cause tensions; Fourth Congress of Czechoslovak Writer's Union meets and denounces anti-Israel policy.

September—Alexander Dubček denounces government's policies on economy and toward Slovaks and intellectuals.

November—Novotný urged to resign, but refuses.

1968 *January 4–5*—Novotný resigns as first secretary of Communist party and is replaced by Dubček.

February—Press censorship disappears in Czechoslovakia, and secret police dismantled.

February 1—Dubček announces "Action Program" for reform.

February 6—Party announces open meetings at which criticism and free discussion will be permitted.

February 11—An economist denounces unfair economic ties with U.S.S.R.

March—"Action Program" discussed at open meetings all over nation; Boy Scouts reestablished; Ban on mention of founder and president of First Czechoslovak Republic, Tomáš Masaryk, is lifted; Ludvík Svoboda replaces Novotný as president.

April—Conservative Czechoslovak Communists begin to plan Dubček's overthrow.

May—U.S.S.R. announces Warsaw Pact maneuvers to be held in Czechoslovakia; Strongly anti-Dubček propaganda campaign begins in Moscow; Kosygin flies to Prague to ask for end of experiment.

June—"Two Thousand Word" proclamation issued by intellectuals; Soviet troops begin maneuvers in Czechoslovakia.

July 8—Dubček ordered to meeting in Warsaw, but refuses to attend.

July 23—Soviet Union announces large-scale maneuvers on Czech-Ukrainian border.

July 29—Meeting of Czechoslovak and Russian leaders at Čierna-nad-Tisou.

August 3—Dubček and other Warsaw Pact leaders meet in Bratislava and pledge "cooperation."

August 18—Invasion ordered by Moscow.

August 20–21—Soviet, Polish, Hungarian, East German, and Bulgarian troops invade Czechoslovakia.

August 22—Czechoslovak Communist party holds secret congress in Prague; Underground radio goes into operation to keep public informed.

August 23—Svoboda flies to Moscow to win release of Dubček and other leaders.

Autumn—Soviet Union imposes "normalization" on Czechoslovakia.

1969 *April 17*—Dubček resigns and is replaced as first secretary by Gustav Husák.

Other Books to Read

Chapman, Colin. *August 21st: The Rape of Czechoslovakia.* London: Cassell, 1968.

Glaser, Kurt. *Czechoslovakia: A Critical History.* Caldwell, Idaho: The Caxton Printers, 1961.

Gluckstein, Ygael. *Stalin's Satellites in Europe.* London: George Allen and Unwin, 1952.

Journalist M. *A Year is Eight Months.* Introduction by Tad Szulc. Garden City, New York: Doubleday, 1970.

Kennan, George F. *From Prague After Munich: Diplomatic Papers 1938–1940.* Princeton: Princeton University Press, 1968.

Kohout, Pavel. *From the Diary of a Counter-Revolutionary.* New York: McGraw-Hill, 1972.

Korbel, Josef. *The Communist Subversion of Czechoslovakia 1938–1948: The Failure of Coexistence.* Princeton: Princeton University Press, 1959.

Littell, Robert, ed. *The Czech Black Book.* New York: Frederick A. Praeger, 1959.

Mňačko, Ladislav. *The Seventh Night.* New York: E. P. Dutton, 1969.

Reisky de Dubinic, Vladimir. *Communist Propaganda Methods: A Case Study in Czechoslovakia.* New York: Frederick A. Praeger, 1960.

Rothkopf, Carol Zeman. *Czechoslovakia: A First Book.* New York: Franklin Watts, 1974.

Salomon, M. *The Strangled Revolution.* Boston: Little, Brown, 1971.

Schwartz, Harry. *Prague's 200 Days.* New York: Frederick A. Praeger, 1969.

Szulc, Tad. *Czechoslovakia Since World War II.* New York: Viking, 1971.

Taborsky, Edward. *Communism in Czechoslovakia: 1948–1960.* Princeton: Princeton University Press, 1961.

Wechsberg, Joseph. *The Voices: Prague 1968.* Garden City, New York: Doubleday, 1969.
Weisskopf, Kurt. *The Agony of Czechoslovakia '38/'68.* London: Elek Books, 1968.
Zeman, Z. A. B. *Prague Spring: A Report on Czechoslovakia 1968.* New York: Hill & Wang, 1969.

Index

About the Author

TAD SZULC was born in Warsaw, Poland and educated in Switzerland and Brazil. During two decades as a journalist with "The New York Times," he reported the news from forty countries. Since 1973 he has been a Washington-based free-lance writer. His experiences in Czechoslovakia are recorded in *Czechoslovakia Since World War II,* as well as in this volume. Among his other books are *Twilight of the Tyrants, The Winds of Revolution, Dominican Diary, Latin America, The Bombs of Palomares, Portrait of Spain,* and *Innocents at Home*. Mr. Szulc is married and the father of two children.